If You Were An Astronaut

By Dinah L. Moché, Ph.D.

All photographs and artists conceptions were provided courtesy of the National Aeronautics and Space Administration (NASA) and Rockwell International Space Operations.

The author wishes to extend special thanks to Rebecca A. Rozen, Harvard-Radcliffe; Dr. Elizabeth K. Rozen, SUNY/Downstate Medical School; Dr. Charles Bourland, Astronaut Roy Bridges, Billie A. Deason, Mike Gentry, Dan Germany, Frances E. Hughes, Dr. James S. Logan, Joyce Rando, Astronaut Dick Scobee, Liza Vasquez, NASA Johnson Space Center, Houston, Texas; Althea Washington, NASA Headquarters, Washington D.C.; Sue Cometa, Robert Howard, Rockwell International Space Operations, Downey, CA.

A GOLDEN BOOK · NEW YORK
Western Publishing Company, Inc., Racine, Wisconsin 53404

If you were an astronaut you'd rocket to space. People and things float freely in space because they weigh nothing. That's called being in zero g. Floating in water feels a lot like being in zero g. So first you'd practice space jobs in a giant pool on Earth.

What is it like to live and work in space? Come aboard a space shuttle and see.

Before launch you are strapped in your seat, lying on your back 147 feet up. The three main engines roar. The shuttle jerks and your heart pounds.

The two solid rocket boosters fire. The ground trembles and the air cracks. The shuttle shakes a lot. Seconds later it lifts off.

**THE EXTERNAL FUEL
TANK SEPARATES**

**SOLID ROCKET
BOOSTERS DROP**

The boosters drop to the ocean to be picked up and used again. Now your ride is smooth.

As you climb faster you feel three times heavier than usual. That's called undergoing 3 g's. It feels as if there is a rock on your chest. (1 g is your normal weight on Earth, or gravity's pull here.)

The main engines shut down and the empty fuel tank destructs. Two small engines fire. Just 10 minutes after you leave Earth you're in orbit 200 miles up.

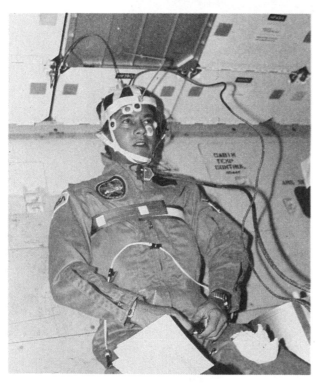

The shuttle zips all around the earth every 90 minutes. Your speed in orbit is 17,500 mph. The crew has a commander who is in charge of the mission, a pilot to help, a mission specialist who manages equipment, and four payload specialists who do experiments.

People live and work in a small cabin up front. There the air is like Earth's. On top is the flight deck with over 2,000 flight controls and 10 windows. The mid-deck is like a camper for living. The lower deck has equipment for clean air and water.

SPACELAB

PAYLOAD BAY

CREW CABIN
WITH FLIGHT DECK

PAYLOAD
BAY DOORS

When you're in zero g strange things happen. You get taller. Blood shifts from your legs to your upper body. That shrinks your thighs and waist, fattens your arms, and puffs your face. It fills your head and stuffs your nose, like a little cold.

Pens, pencils, scissors, and other tools would float if you let them go. Your flight suit has lots of zip-up pockets to keep them in.

Before flying you pack clothes, the way you do when you go camping. You take enough underwear, socks, and shirts so you can change every day. You bring your laundry back to Earth.

There are different meals for each day of the week. You have about 70 foods and 20 drinks with you, plus snacks such as cookies, candy, and gum. Many are dried or heated to keep them from spoiling. There's no refrigerator on the shuttle.

When it's your turn to prepare dinner, you warm frankfurters and potato patties in the oven. You squirt water into dried strawberries and punch. Then you snap the food containers into trays.

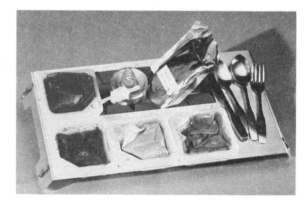

To eat, you fasten your tray to your lap, open the containers, and put a straw in the punch.

Afterward, you clean your silverware and tray to use again.

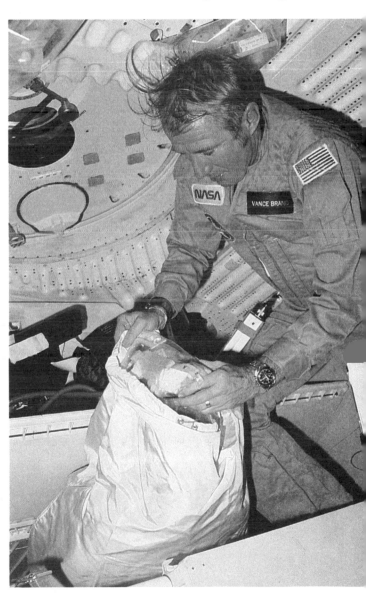

Staying in zero g weakens you like a long stay in bed. You exercise to stay fit. You have one hour a day to put on shorts, work out, and then change again.

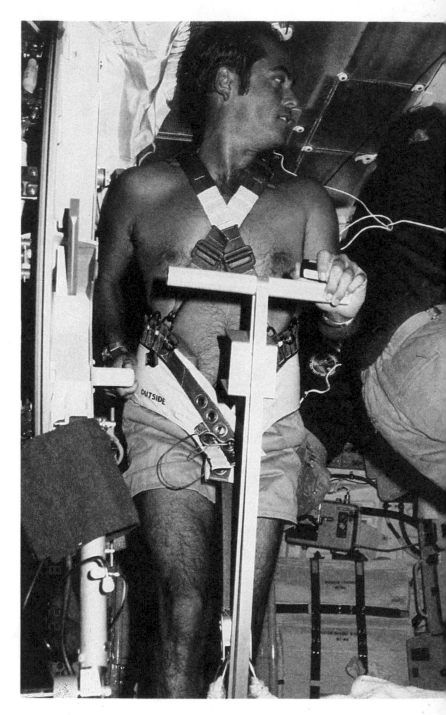

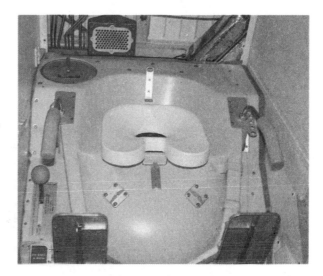

The tiny bathroom has only a toilet. Thigh bars keep you from floating off the seat. There's no room for a sink, bathtub, or shower, so you use a wet washcloth with soap to clean yourself. You spit into a washcloth after brushing your teeth with toothpaste.

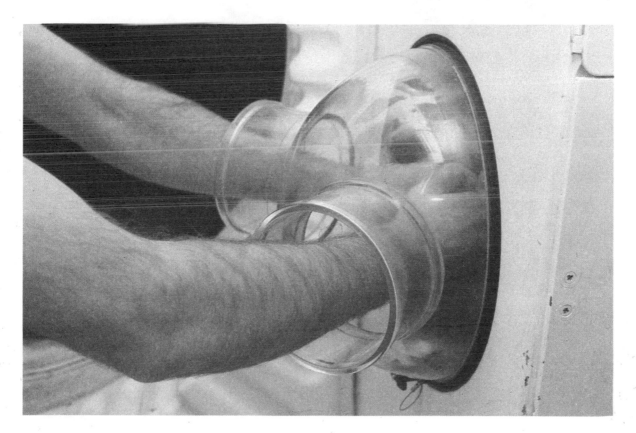

Astronauts work 16 hours a day in orbit. Space shuttles carry freight to and from space. To lift things out of the payload bay or grab things back from space, you operate the robot arm.

You also do experiments to find out what happens to humans, animals, and plants in zero g, and whether new products can be made in space to improve life on Earth.

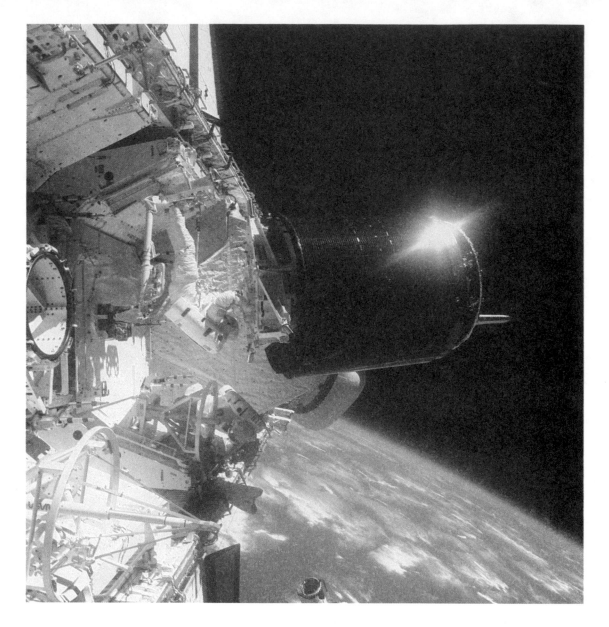

Sometimes you go out of the shuttle to inspect the craft, to service equipment, or to take pictures. But space has dangers—no air to breathe, extreme heat (250°F) and cold (–250°F), deadly rays, and bits of rock (meteoroids) that can hit you like bullets. A spacesuit keeps you safe.

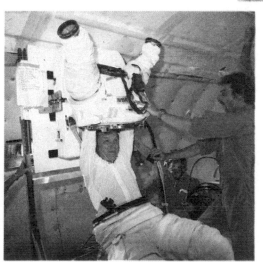

The backpack on the spacesuit has supplies to keep you alive for seven hours. There is a microphone and earphones inside the helmet. A one-person rocket unit that snaps onto the backpack lets you fly around by yourself.

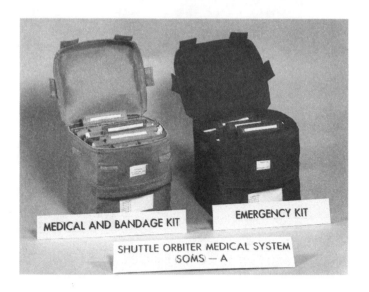

MEDICAL AND BANDAGE KIT   EMERGENCY KIT

SHUTTLE ORBITER MEDICAL SYSTEM
SOMS — A

There's a medical kit on board in case you get sick or hurt. It has thermometers, aspirins, syringes, stethoscopes, iodine, bandages, and drugs. When you need a doctor you can talk to one at Mission Control by radio.

If a minor shuttle part fails, a backup part takes over the job. If this also fails, a third is ready. You must land right away if an engine breaks.

A rescue craft can pick up a stranded crew. Two astronauts in spacesuits transfer the others to the craft in big plastic balls that have earthlike air inside.

The busy crew has no play time. For fun you test how things like food act in zero g, listen to music, and look out the windows. You can see mountains, lakes, green forests, sandy deserts, cities, airfields, and highways on Earth.

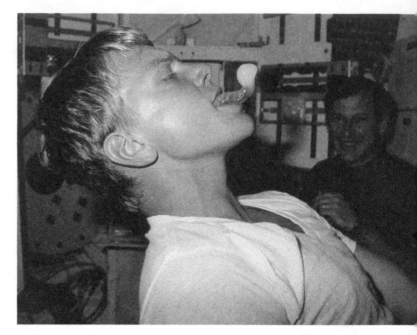

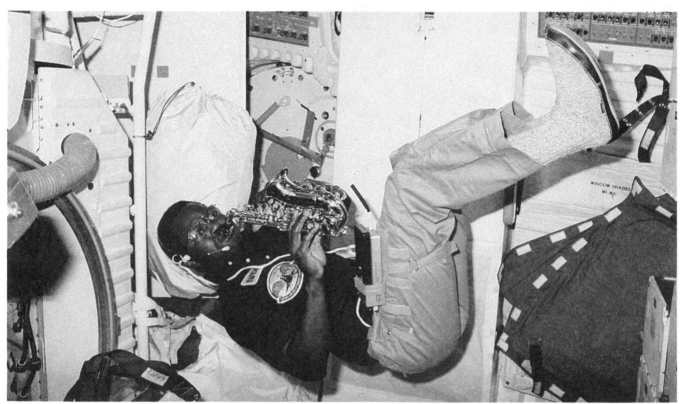

Eight hours are scheduled for sleep. Although you're too excited to be sleepy, you put away your outer clothes and shoes. Then you zip yourself into a sleep sack that is clipped to a wall so you won't drift and bump into things. Eyeshades and earplugs shut out light and noise.

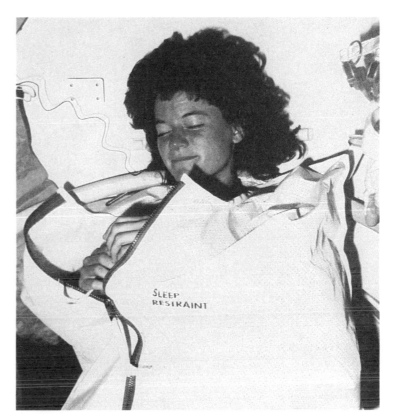

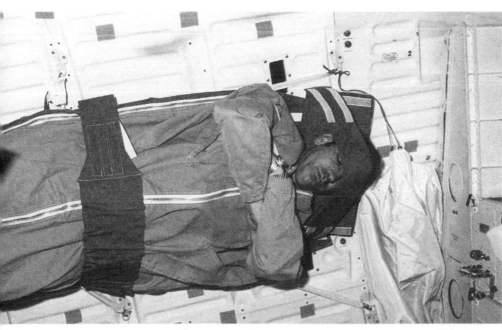

When your mission is over you get set to land. The air gets fiery when the shuttle plunges through it toward Earth. Extra g's pull blood from your brain to your lower body as you slow down quickly. You wear an anti-g suit to squeeze it back up so you don't faint.

With the engines off, the shuttle glides to Earth.

Trucks roll out to cool the shuttle and to supply electrical power. Meanwhile you shut down systems and put away gear.

Then you exit to a van. You clean up, get a medical checkup, and relax for a day. Finally you are debriefed—you tell space scientists everything you learned on your mission.

Soon astronauts will fly missions in a space station that circles Earth. People, supplies, and equipment will be shuttled up as needed. The astronauts will live in the space station and explore for months. Will you join a crew?